ZERO

IS IT SOMETHING? IS IT NOTHING?

by Claudia Zaslavsky
pictures by Jeni Bassett

Franklin Watts
New York London Toronto Sydney
1989

To Clara and David,
who know that something is not nothing

C.Z.

Library of Congress Cataloging-in-Publication Data

Zaslavsky, Claudia.
    Zero : is it something? is it nothing? / by Claudia Zaslavsky :
illustrated by Jeni Bassett.
        p.   cm.—(Discovering science)
    Summary: Discusses the meaning and mathematical possibilities of
the number zero.
    ISBN 0-531-10693-4
    1. Zero (The number)—Juvenile literature.   [1. Zero (The number)
2. Number concept.]   I. Bassett, Jeni, ill.   II. Title.
III. Series: Discovering science (Franklin Watts, Inc.)
QA141.3.Z37   1989
513'.5—dc19   88-38940   CIP   AC

Text copyright © 1989 by Claudia Zaslavsky
Illustrations copyright © 1989 by Jeni Bassett
Printed in the United States of America

How many animals are on the chair?
How many animals are on Sandy's bed?
How many animals are under the bed?

Sandy counted 2 animals on the chair.
She counted 4 animals on the bed.
She found NO animals under the bed.
NONE AT ALL.
The number is 0. ZERO.

How many children are at the party?
How many elephants are at the party?

Sandy and Joe invited 5 friends to the party.
There are 7 children in all.

Sandy and Joe did not invite any elephants.
There are NO elephants at the party.
NONE AT ALL.
The number of elephants is 0. ZERO.

How many markers are in the box?
How many markers are white?

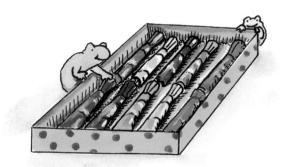

There are 10 markers in the box.
5 are in one row and 5 in the other row.
NO marker is white. Not a single one.
NONE AT ALL.
The number is 0. ZERO.

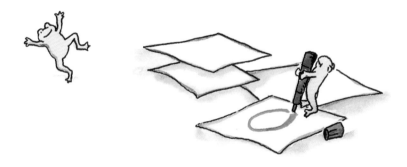

What does ZERO mean?

Sometimes zero means NOTHING.
How many animals were under Sandy's bed? 0
How many elephants were at the party? 0
How many white markers were in the box? 0

Hold up 4 fingers.

Can you find another way?

Hold up 7 fingers.

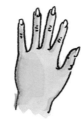 

Can you find another way?

Hold up 10 fingers.

 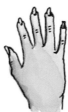

Can you find another way?

Hold up 0 fingers.

How many different ways can you do that?

Sometimes zero means SOMETHING.

How many fingers are on two hands?

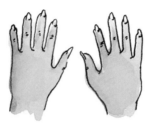

We can write the number.   10

Cross out the zero,   1⦸
and you have
1

10 and 1 are different numbers.
In the number 10, zero means something.

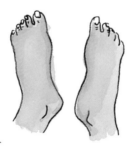

You have twenty fingers and toes.

We can write the number.   20
Now cross out the zero.   2⦸
2 fingers and toes! How silly!

In the number 20, zero means something.

Some numbers have zero in the middle.

Joe lives at 205 Maple Street.
Cross out the zero.   2Ø5
You won't find Joe at 25 Maple Street.

This zero means something.

Some numbers end in two zeros, like 100.

Cross out one zero.   10Ø
Cross out two zeros.   1ØØ
The number is different each time.

These zeros mean something.

Count the pennies.
Ten pennies in each pile.
Ten piles. Count by tens:
10, 20, 30, 40, 50, 60, 70, 80, 90, 100.
One hundred pennies in all.

How are these numbers alike?
They all end in zero.
Do these zeros mean something?
If you cross out the zeros, you have different numbers.

These zeros mean something.

ROUND NUMBERS

Mike and Zubin are going
   to play with their marbles.
Mike thinks that he has
   about 30 marbles
   in his bag.

Is 30 a good guess?

He rolls them out on the ground.
Mike and Zubin count the marbles.
32 marbles were in the bag.
32 is close to 30.

30 is a good guess.

A queen bee may lay about one million eggs during her
  lifetime.
No one has actually counted all the eggs.
1,000,000 is a good guess.

30 ends in zero. 1,000,000 ends in zeros.
People may use such numbers when they don't know
  EXACTLY how many.
Numbers that end in zeros are often called ROUND
  numbers.
Round numbers only tell ABOUT how many.

Ask the letter carrier how many letters
  he has delivered.
Do you think he knows EXACTLY how many?

SOMETIMES O IS A NUMBER.
SOMETIMES O IS A LETTER.

Look at the signs.
Find the letter O. The letter is called OH.
Find the number 0. The number is called ZERO.

Carlos needs help to make a phone call.
To call the operator, he presses 0.
0 means OPERATOR.
0 also means ZERO.

How do you read this license plate?
Sometimes it's hard to know.

THE ODOMETER

Maria has a new bike.
It has a counter called an odometer (*oh-DOM-eater*).
The odometer counts the number of miles the bike has
    gone.

When Maria got the bike,
    the odometer looked like this:
Four digits, all zeros.

Now the odometer looks like this:
How many miles has the bike gone?
Thirty miles.

Soon the odometer will look like this:

Ninety-nine miles!
What number will show up next?
(*For the answer, turn the page.*)

One hundred miles!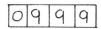

What comes after this number?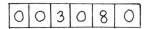

The next time you are in the front seat of a car, look at
   the odometer.
Try to read the number of miles the car has gone.
This counter shows six digits:

How many miles has the car traveled?
Which zeros mean something?
Which zeros mean nothing?

You can make a counter.
You will need:
   A sheet of heavy paper.
   Four strips of heavy paper, each one 1 inch
      wide and 11 inches long.
   Sticky tape, scissors, marker or pen, ruler.
Ask a grown-up to help you.

On each strip of paper:

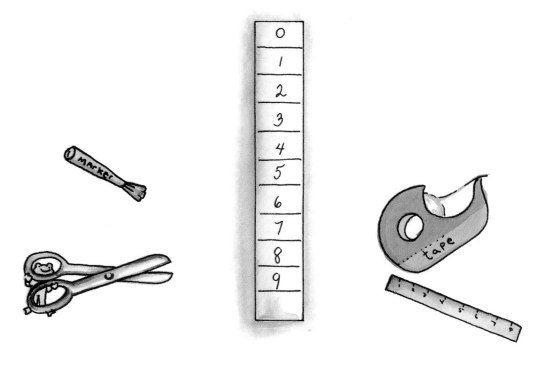

Mark off eleven equal spaces by drawing ten lines,
   1 inch apart. Write the numbers 0 through 9.
Leave the last space empty.

On the sheet of paper:

Rule four 2-inch wide columns. Into each column, cut two slits, as shown in the diagram, 1 inch wide and 1 inch apart.

Write the headings:

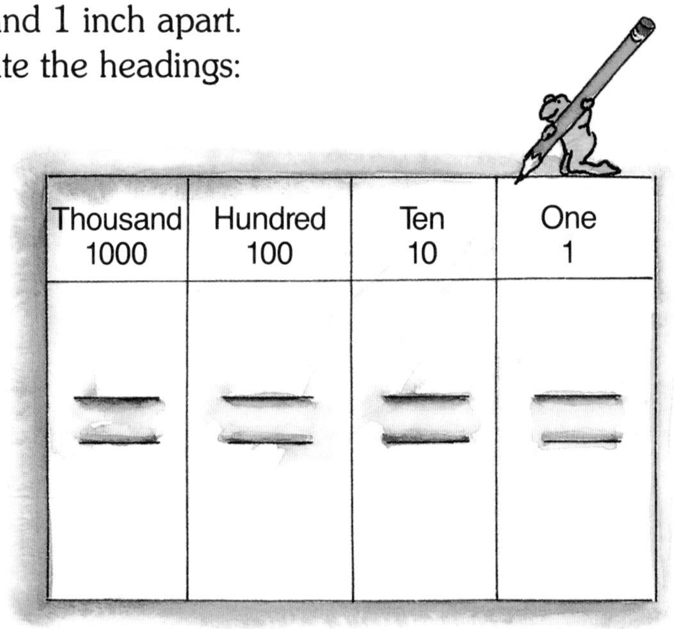

Thousand 1000	Hundred 100	Ten 10	One 1
=	=	=	=

Push one strip of paper through each pair of slits in each column.

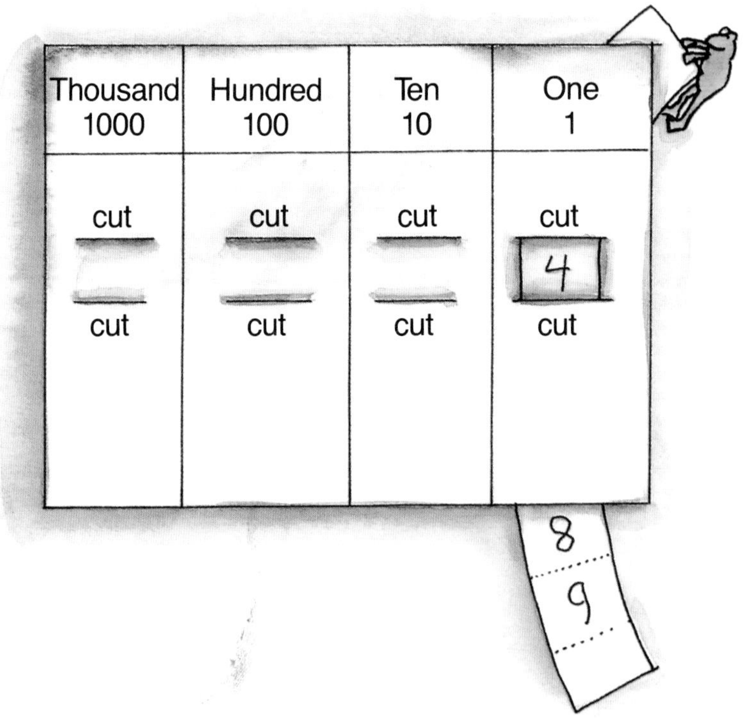

Thousand 1000	Hundred 100	Ten 10	One 1
cut	cut	cut	cut
			4
cut	cut	cut	cut

8
9

Tape the zero over the empty space so that the strip becomes a loop.

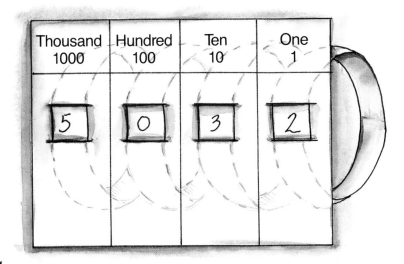

Now you can show any number from zero to nine thousand, nine hundred ninety-nine.

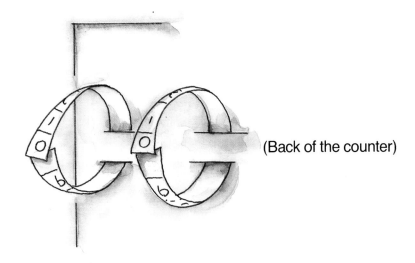

(Back of the counter)

ZERO IS A FUNNY NUMBER

Kazu is counting her money.
She has four coins in one hand.
She has NO coins in the other hand.
She has four coins in all.
FOUR plus ZERO equals FOUR.
$$4 + 0 = 4$$

Ian had two apples.
He ate one apple and John ate the other.
How many apples are left?
NO apples are left.
The answer is ZERO.
TWO minus TWO equals ZERO.
$$2 - 2 = 0$$

Nothing is in the first glass.
Nothing is in the second glass.
Nothing is in the third glass.
Three times nothing is nothing.
THREE times ZERO equals ZERO.

$$3 \times 0 = 0$$

Sandy planned to buy five party favors for her five guests.
But Sandy forgot to buy them.
There were NO party favors.
How many party favors did each child get?
Nothing divided by five is nothing.
ZERO divided by FIVE equals ZERO.

$$0 \div 5 = 0$$

Sometimes ZERO means NOTHING.

Sometimes ZERO means SOMETHING.

ALL KINDS OF MEASURES

Ben and Sarah are baking cookies.
Ben puts the sheet of cookies into the oven.
Then Sarah sets the timer to ring in 15 minutes.
At the end of 15 minutes the pointer is at ZERO.
There is NO time left.

Chen is making a kite.
He measures with a ruler.
Measuring starts from ZERO.
Chen doesn't see zero marked on the ruler.
Where should ZERO be on the ruler?

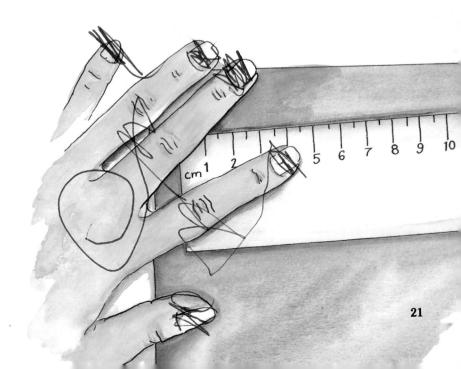

Olga has new ice skates.
Will the pond freeze over soon?
Look at the thermometer.

The temperature is just ZERO.
Water turns to ice when
   the temperature is just ZERO.
Olga hopes that she
   will be able to skate
   tomorrow.

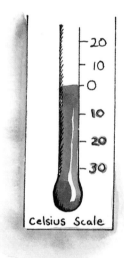

COUNTDOWN: 9, 8, 7, 6, 5, 4, 3, 2, 1.
Blast off on ZERO!
Soon the spaceship is in orbit around the Earth.

The astronauts are floating in the spaceship.
The gravity of the earth pulls things toward the Earth.
It keeps people from floating away from the Earth.

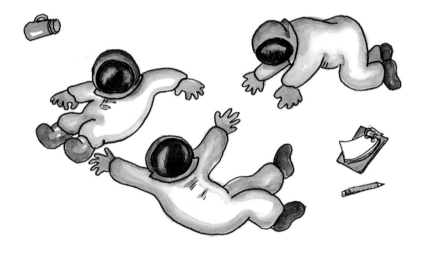

But when the astronauts are in orbit, they do not feel
    the pull of gravity.
They are living with ZERO GRAVITY.
The astronauts weigh nothing at all.
They are weightless.
Their weight is ZERO.

ZERO HAS OTHER NAMES!
Do you know the name for ZERO in another language?
Spanish people say CERO.
In Russian the word is NOOL.
In Arabic the word is SIFR.

David and Clara are playing tennis.
The score is THIRTY–LOVE.
Clara has 30 points.
David has NO Points.
In tennis, LOVE is another name for ZERO.

LOVE sounds like the French word L'OEUF, pronounced
    LUF.
It means THE EGG.
A zero looks like an egg.

Efua and Molly like to play NOUGHTS (pronounced "nawts") AND CROSSES.
Maybe you call the game TIC-TAC-TOE.
NOUGHT is another name for ZERO.
Two people play the game.
Each player tries to get three marks in a row.
One player makes noughts, the other makes crosses.

Molly goes first. Her mark is 0, called NOUGHT.
Efua's mark is X, called CROSS.
Molly won this game.

WHO WROTE THE FIRST ZERO?
We think the Maya people were the first
   to write a zero, many hundred of years ago.
Their zero looked like a shell.
The Maya live in Central America, in the countries
   of Mexico, Guatemala, and Belize.

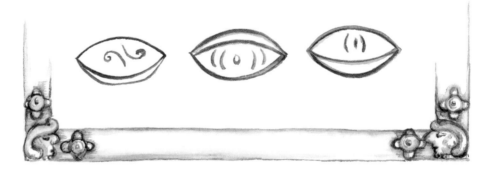

Halfway around the world live the Hindu people of India. They invented a sign for zero many hundreds of years ago.

The Arabs brought the Hindu number system to other lands.

That is why the numbers we write are called Hindu-Arabic numerals.

Zero has been written in different ways:

The Maya wrote   The Hindus wrote   o

Now we write   ◯

The calculator shows   *0*   Some computers print   Ø

RIDDLES

Can you guess the answers to the riddles?

(Answers are on page 32.)

1. I am a huge enormous number,
    Seven digits, plain to see.
    But if you were to rub out one,
    Nothing would be left of me.

    What number am I?

28

2. 10,000,000,000,000,000,000,000,000,000,000,0
00,000,000,000,000,000,000,000,000,000,000,0
00,000,000,000,000,000,000,000,000.
Guess how many zeros are in this number.

3. I'm thinking of a number.
Can you guess its name?
When multiplied by another,
It always stays the same.
Divide it by two, by five, by six,
The answer is again
The number that you started with.
Can you name it, then?

RICKY: Do you know what, Jane? There were ghosts in
         our house last night!
JANE: Ghosts, Ricky? Our house has ten times as many
         ghosts as yours!

Who is telling the truth?
Who is not telling the truth?

Ricky is not telling the truth. He is teasing Jane.
Ricky knows that there are no ghosts.
Ricky's house has ZERO ghosts.

Jane is telling the truth.
Ten times ZERO is ZERO.
Jane's house has ZERO ghosts, too.

How many ghosts have you seen in your house?

Answers to riddles on pages 28 and 29:

1. I am the number 1,000,000.
   Erase the 1. Only zeros remain.

2. One hundred zeros.
   A nine-year-old boy made up a name for this number.
   He called it a GOOGOL.
   Now everyone calls this number a googol.
   A googol is written:
   ONE followed by one hundred ZEROS.

3. The number is ZERO.